hip . . .

HOORAY!

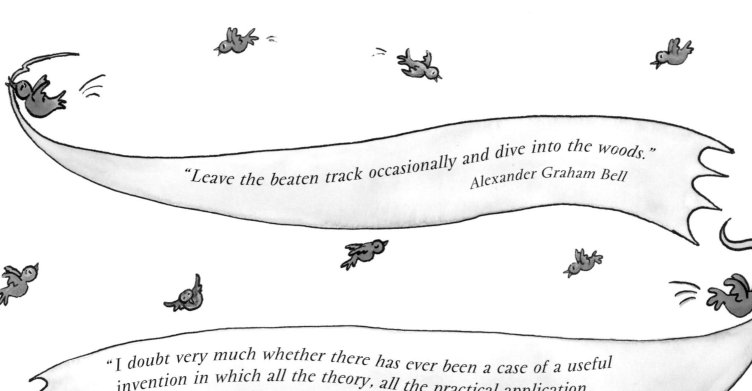

"*Leave the beaten track occasionally and dive into the woods.*"
Alexander Graham Bell

"*I doubt very much whether there has ever been a case of a useful invention in which all the theory, all the practical application, and all the apparatus were the work of one man.*"
Guglielmo Marconi

First U.S. edition 2005

Library of Congress Cataloging-in-Publication Data

Williams, Marcia, date.
Hooray for inventors! /Marcia Williams. —1st U.S. ed.
p. cm.
Includes index.
ISBN 0-7636-2760-7
1. Inventors—United States—Biography—Juvenile literature. I. Title.
T39.W542 2005
609.2'2—dc22   2005046915

10 9 8 7 6 5 4 3 2 1

Printed in China

This book was typeset in Vendome.
The illustrations were done in watercolor and ink.

Candlewick Press
2067 Massachusetts Avenue
Cambridge, Massachusetts 02140

visit us at www.candlewick.com

# HOORAY
## FOR
# INVENTORS!

## Marcia Williams

CANDLEWICK PRESS
CAMBRIDGE, MASSACHUSETTS

# Let's Hear It for Leonardo da Vinci!

THIS BOOK IS DEDICATED TO MY
SPECIAL HERO OF INVENTION,

## Leonardo da Vinci

♥ (1452 ~1519) ♥

So, what did he invent?

Cast your eyes yonder and you will see a few of the many inventions.

LEONARDO DA VINCI was born in Italy during the Renaissance, a time of learning and creativity in Europe. He was a brilliant artist and a great inventor, though many of his inventions were so advanced that they would have to be reinvented hundreds of years later when technology had caught up with them. Some of Leonardo's inventions were inspired by his study of nature, such as his airplane with flapping wings. He produced beautiful technical drawings of his experiments and observations, which still astound and inspire scientists today. Leonardo was also a gentle, peace-loving vegetarian, who bought caged birds just for the joy of setting them free!

*THANK YOU, SIGNOR DA VINCI, FOR YOUR INSPIRATION!*

Thank you, Signor da Vinci, for our freedom!

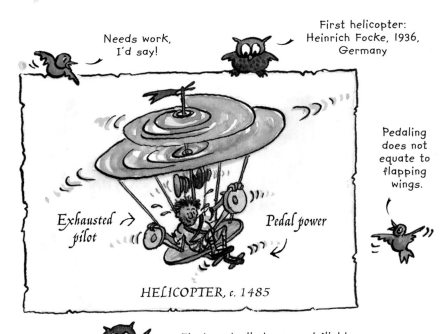

# All Praise the Reader!

I thought we were praising inventors!

Readers are important too!

There would be no readers without inventors.

First alphabet: Phoenicians, c. 1700 BC

There would be no date today without the inventors of yesterday.

Calendar: Ancient Rome, 45 BC

Dear Reader,

This is a book about my favorite inventors, my personal heroes and heroines of invention. Before I started writing this book, I imagined that inventors were boring, eccentric scientists who never left their laboratories. I was wrong. Inventors come in all shapes, sizes, sexes, and ages, and they are brilliant. Well, most of them are brilliant!

Inventors don't just discover things that have always been there but have gone unnoticed; they create things that are entirely new. They see a need for something and then work away until they find the solution, although not all inventors are totally original. Some take an invention that isn't working very well and reinvent it so that it works superbly and everybody wants it! An invention that nobody wants soon gets forgotten, while other inventions change our lives forever.

Every generation has had inventors. Every generation will have inventors. Perhaps there is an inventor lurking inside you. Without inventors, we might still be living in the Stone Age.

HOORAY FOR INVENTORS!
I hope you enjoy reading about them.

Marcia Williams

P.S. If you do become an inventor, don't forget to patent your information. A patent will stop other inventors from stealing your idea and gives you the sole right to make and sell your invention.

P.P.S. The words the inventors and others use in this book are not their own. I have taken the liberty of imagining what they might have said.

So, who are the chosen inventors?

Do we need to know?

Allow us to present . . .

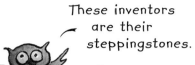
Why aren't there more modern inventors listed?

These inventors are their steppingstones.

Without the radio, no TV.

Without the TV, no video.

Without the video, no DVD.

# Contents

Hooray for Johannes Gutenberg (1400–1468) and His Movable Type . . . . . . . 10

Thanks, James Watt (1736–1819), for the Separate Steam Condenser . . . . . . . 12

Toot-Toot-Toot-Toot for Richard Trevithick (1771–1833),
George Stephenson (1781–1848), and the Steam Railroad . . . . . . . . . . . . . . 14

Light Up for Thomas Edison (1847–1931) . . . . . . . . . . . . . . . . . . . . . 16

Put Your Hands Together for Inventors of Useful Things . . . . . . . . . . . . . . 18

Ring Those Bells for Antonio Meucci (1808–1889),
Alexander Graham Bell (1847–1922), and the Telephone . . . . . . . . . . . . . . 20

Three Zooms for Wilbur Wright (1867–1912),
Orville Wright (1871–1948), and Their Fabulous Flying Machine . . . . . . . . . . 24

Viva, Guglielmo Marconi (1874–1937) and His Radio . . . . . . . . . . . . . . . 28

Tune In for John Logie Baird (1888–1946) and the TV Boys . . . . . . . . . . . . 30

Extra-Loud Cheers for Women Inventors . . . . . . . . . . . . . . . . . . . . . . 32

And Finally, My Favorite Inventors, Take a Bow . . . . . . . . . . . . . . . . . . 34

Index of Inventors . . . . . . . . . . . . . . . . . . . . . . . . . . . . . . . . . 36

Index of Inventions . . . . . . . . . . . . . . . . . . . . . . . . . . . . . . . . 37

We don't want DVDs. We like videos.

You two have no sense of adventure.

Just think where a DVD might lead to.

Can I have a DVD?

Here we go . . . consumer-itis!

Pi Sheng from China invented movable type in AD 1041.

Well, it never reached Europe, so it needed reinventing!

Lucky for him, paper had been invented!

Paper: AD 105, China

Ink: 2500 BC, China and Egypt

Can owls do jokes or just facts?

Inventions don't come cheap!

Cheap! Cheap! Cheap!

# Hooray for Johannes Gutenberg (1400~1468) and His Movable Type

When Johannes was growing up in Mainz, Germany, nobody read him a bedtime story because there were no books to read.

The only book Johannes ever saw was the Bible. He would watch the monks at the local monastery copying it by hand. The only known method of printing then was woodblock printing, and that was very slow.

When he was older, Johannes trained as a goldsmith and went to work in a mint, where coins were struck.

While he stamped out the coins, he had an idea of casting individual letters for printing in a similar way.

But the tools, inks, and metals he needed were very expensive.

For a while, three bankers helped him out with money.

Then one died, and the other two tried to steal his plans.

If purses hadn't been invented, they couldn't be empty.

If my tummy hadn't been invented, it couldn't be empty.

*My dreams are shattered.*

**Johannes was forced to give up his experiments.**

*As much as you want. Pay me back when you're rich and famous.*

*Really?*

**Then Johann Fust, a lawyer, lent him the money to start again.**

*I'm ready! The moment has come to print the first Gutenberg Bible.*

**By 1450, Johannes had cast the letters and prepared a printing press.**

*Before you begin, I'd like my money back, PLUS a lot of interest, NOW!*

*You're joking!*

**But then, Fust asked for his money back, with interest!**

*My purse is empty.*

*You must have something of value.*

**Poor Johannes had spent it all on the press.**

*Ah, yes, your press. Thank you, my dear fellow.*

*No!*

**He was forced to hand over his press and work for Fust.**

*More ink coming up, Mr. Gutenberg!*

*I'll have to learn to read now, Mr. Gutenberg!*

*Those are my Bibles!*

PAGES WAITING FOR BINDING

INK AS USED BY PAINTERS

FORM FOR ARRANGING LETTERS

METAL LETTERS

LETTERS

PRESS ADAPTED FROM OLIVE OR GRAPE PRESS

VELLUM BEING STRETCHED

*Yes, but now the stories belong to everyone.*

*Will you read me a story?*

**But Johannes still achieved his childhood dream. In 1456, while employed by Fust, he started to print his first Bible. It could take a monk up to thirty years to make one copy of the Bible. In one year, Johannes had printed 300 copies! By 1500, there were printers all over Europe and they had printed 30,000 books. As a result, knowledge and change spread with increasing speed.**

What he needs is a patent!

Birdbrain! Modern patents weren't invented until 1625.

Owls think they are so clever.

I'm not in a position to comment.

Three cheers for the Gutenberg Bible!

It was an information revolution!

Imagine having to learn to read.

It boggles the mind.

11

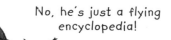
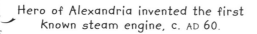
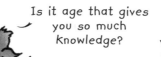

# THANKS, JAMES WATT (1736–1819), for the SEPARATE STEAM CONDENSER

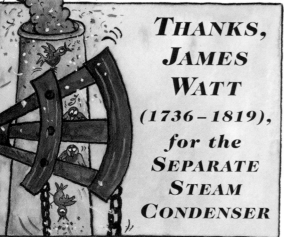

James Watt was born in Greenock, a small Scottish fishing village. He was a clever boy, but too sickly to go to school, so he stayed at home tinkering with this and that.

When he did go to school, he was a top student, but his attendance was very poor.

Eventually, James got a job at Glasgow University making and repairing scientific instruments.

One day, a friend brought him a model of a Newcomen steam engine to repair.

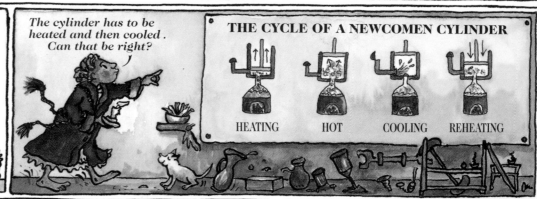

James had heard of this engine. It was named after its inventor, Thomas Newcomen, and was used for pumping water out of mines. It was a smart idea, but it did not work very efficiently.

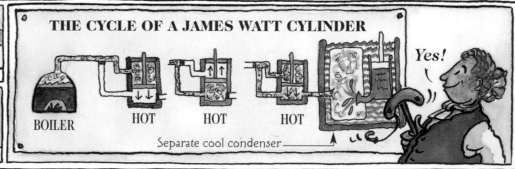

James went for a little walk and had big thoughts. Before long, he realized that he could improve the engine by making a separate cool container in which the steam would condense on its own.

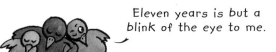

**But James could not raise the money to build his engine. He did jobs he hated for eleven years.**

**At last, he met a businessman, Matthew Boulton, and they formed a partnership.**

**They finally made the James Watt engine in 1776. It pumped wonderfully, used less fuel than the Newcomen engine, and the miners stayed a lot drier! The new steam engine soon began to make other industries, such as the manufacture of cotton, quicker and more efficient. Watt kept on improving his steam engine until he was so rich he did not have to work anymore. Then he thought he might invent a moving steam engine, but he decided he would rather go back to tinkering with this and that.**

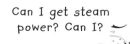

Speaking of rails . . .

Actually, the Ancient Greeks shifted theater scenery on rails.

Richard was a Cornish mining engineer. George was from Newcastle, England.

## Toot-Toot-Toot-Toot
### for Richard Trevithick (1771–1833),
### George Stephenson (1781–1848),
### and the STEAM RAILROAD

Out you go. You are too slow, too obstinate, and too big!

Yes, sir!

I want to be a wrestler.

No, Son. It's the mines for you.

Faster, baby.

Unlike James Watt, Richard Trevithick dreamed of steam transport. He left school early and went to work in the mines with his father. There he worked on the steam engines used to drag wagons of coal on rails.

I need to work on the steering;

One of us needs to lose weight.

Richard built a small high-pressure steam carriage on wheels, but it ran into a house!
Then in 1803, he built a steam locomotive that ran on cast-iron mining rails, but the rails broke.

ONE PENNY A RIDE ON THE TREVITHICK STEAM ENGINE

CATCH ME WHO CAN

Is this a new breed of horse?

It's a wild beast!

It's the work of Satan.

SAY NO TO LOCOS!

Four years later, he built a lighter locomotive that pulled passenger wagons around a circular track. It caused a lot of excitement. But Richard failed to raise the money to develop his idea. Eventually, he gave up and became a mining engineer in Peru.

Batten down the hatches, Son. Here comes a dragon!

Speed can be fatal.

A younger man, George Stephenson, took up the challenge. George had also worked around mines from an early age. He had designed a miner's safety lamp and was a wiz at improving the power of steam engines. He wanted steam locomotives to replace horse-drawn tramways.

His chance came when he was employed by Edward Pease, a businessman who wanted goods transported between two cities.

By 1825, George had two steam locomotives, *Locomotion* and *Hope*, plus a passenger train called *Experiment*, running between the two towns.

Then in 1829, George and his son, Robert, entered and won a competition with their train *Rocket*, which traveled unloaded at the unheard-of speed of 35 mph. The contest convinced the British government that a steam railroad was a good idea. By 1838, George's railroad was running so efficiently that he was able to retire. But he never stopped inventing and always traveled by rail!

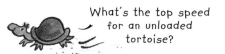

15

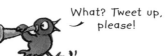 Poor Thomas. He began to go deaf when he was thirteen.

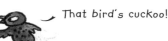 What? Tweet up, please!

That bird's cuckoo!

 Snore!

 He became known as "the wizard" because he invented so many things.

 Like what?

Well, a moving picture machine, a talking doll, a flame-thrower . . .

 What about the telegraph?

 No, that was Claude Chappe, 1793, France. It was replaced by the electric telegraph: Samuel Morse, 1842, USA.

Dot . . . dot . . . dash.

 He'll start another fire — you mark my words.

# LIGHT UP FOR THOMAS EDISON (1847–1931)

LATEST NEWS, SWEETEST SWEETS!

ME! ME!

In 1859, twelve-year-old American Thomas Edison was earning a living selling candy and newspapers on the Ohio railroad line. He enjoyed a healthy profit!

I want those poisons out of my house!

But they are harmless.

You'd think that I was going to blow the place up!

Thomas loved science and had a laboratory at home until he moved it to a railcar for safety.

Oops!

GO AND DON'T COME BACK!

Unfortunately, within weeks, the carriage had been burned to the ground and Thomas had lost his job.

Time to make a move!

He was not out of work for long. Shortly afterward, he saved a little boy from an oncoming train.

Mr. Morse has invented a code of short and long signals to tap out messages on this machine.

So that's how you know when a train is due.

As a reward, the boy's father taught him Morse code and how to use the electric telegraph.

No, sirree, you won't see my hand move, 'cause I'm the fastest operator in the USA!

Thomas quickly became a super-fast operator and was able to travel and work all over America.

Now, if I just unscrew this . . .

add a bit of this . . .

put this here . . .

But he was more interested in selling his ideas for improving the telegraph and similar machines.

If you want to work for me, forget sleep!

Of course, sir—snore!

By 1869, he had made enough money to set up an inventing business in Menlo Park, New Jersey.

 Wanna bet that he'll invent a way to keep 'em awake?

 What, like a night-light?

It was a great time to be an inventor. With a team of assistants, Thomas could invent and even take orders for inventions.

In 1877, he invented the amazing phonograph. It was a forerunner of the record player and recorded sound on a metal cylinder.

But his chief ambition was electric light in every home! For that, he needed to improve the light bulb invented by the Englishman Joseph Swan. It took a while, but Thomas finally succeeded.

Electric light was safer, brighter, and cleaner than gas lamps, and to prove it, in 1879, Thomas threw a public New Year's Eve party. Three thousand people arrived in the dark. . . . Then the lights were switched on! The party was a great success, and everyone left convinced that electric light was the future. Thomas went on to design complete electrical systems. Once that was done, he kept on inventing. He was a true businessman, and his business was inventing!

# Put Your Hands Together for Inventors of Useful Things

*Hands, not feet!*

*Sorry!*

**Left margin notes:**

Hands were invented 'cause people have no beaks!

Can opener: Robert Yeates, 1855, Great Britain

Flush toilet: John Harrington, 1591, Great Britain

He made quite a splash!

The Romans also invented mouthwash made out of urine!

Yuck!

Antiseptics: Ignaz Semmelweis, 1847, Hungary

---

### PHILIBERT DE L'ORME
**Concrete, 1568, France**

*Romans, my foot— we Egyptians invented concrete to build the pyramids!*

*Prove it!*

Concrete was invented by the Romans c. 200 BC. The architect de L'Orme rediscovered it.

---

### PETER DURAND
**Tin Can, 1810, Great Britain**

*Mess up!*

You needed a hammer and chisel to open early tin cans!

---

### WALTER ALCOCK
**Toilet Paper on a Roll, 1882, Great Britain**

*Help!*

*Come and get it!*

*Not guilty!*

---

### LADISLAO BIRO: Ballpoint Pen, 1938, Hungary

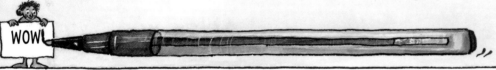

WOW!

More than 14 million ballpoint pens are sold every day!

---

### THE GOOD OLD ROMANS: Toothpaste, c. ages ago!

First toothpaste in a tube: Dr. Washington Sheffield, 1892, USA

The Romans made their toothpaste from wine vinegar and pumice stone.

---

### ROWLAND HILL
**Postage Stamp, 1840, Great Britain**

*Delivery will cost you: 3 sheep, 2 hens, and 1 fish*

*No: 1 sheep, 3 hens, and 1 dormouse. My final offer!*

The Ancient Egyptians had a postal service by 2000 BC, but no stamps!

---

### EARLE DICKSON
**Band-Aid, 1920, USA**

*I'm all cut up!*

*As you see, I had to do something!*

Earle invented Band-Aids for his accident-prone wife.

---

### CLARENCE BIRDSEYE
**Frozen Food, 1924, USA**

*Frozen food!*

*What's new about that?*

---

### GEORGE DE MESTRAL
**Velcro, 1956, Switzerland**

*It was these tight-clinging cocklebur seeds that gave me the idea!*

*Persistent little seeds!*

---

Why eat canned or frozen food when you can eat fresh food?

People are addicted to convenience.

## MASARU IBUKA
### Walkman, 1979, Japan

Even parents use them!

## RANDOLPH SMITH and KENNETH HOUSE
### Smoke Alarm, 1969, USA

*WAA!*      *WAA!*

*Oops, I'm on fire!*

*Every day that noise saves thousands of lives!*

## STEVE JOBS and STEPHEN WOZNIAK
### Personal Computer, 1977, USA

Small, fast computers were made possible by the invention of integrated circuits or silicon chips, which were first built in 1958 and 1959 by JACK KILBY and ROBERT NOYCE, USA.

All I need is an air current to play on.

## GIDEON SUNDBACK
### Zipper, 1913, USA

First invented by Whitcomb Judson in 1893. But it didn't work then, and if you ask me, it doesn't work now . . . OUCH!

## TIM BERNERS-LEE
### World Wide Web, 1990, Great Britain

Tim's computer program called Enquire Within Upon Everything allowed everyone to use the Internet with just a click of a mouse.

### DOUG ENGELBART
Computer Mouse, 1965, USA

*Eeeek!*

## HUBERT BOOTH
### Vacuum Cleaner, 1901, Great Britain

*Thanks to Mr. Booth, kids do their chores and have time to put their feet up.*

*Up!*

*Up!*

*Up!*

## ALESSANDRO DI SPINA and SALVINO DEGLI ARMATI
### Eyeglasses, c. 1280, Italy

*All the better to see you with, my dear!*

Yeah, I'm a real high flyer!

### PETER HENLEIN
Watch, 1500, Germany

| BEFORE | AFTER |
|---|---|
| *So lovely to see you.* | *You're late!* |

**Button, c. 1235, Germany**

*Oops, a lost button!*

### BELL TELEPHONE LABS
Mobile Phone, 1947, USA

*Was there life before the mobile phone?*

*Are you crazy? Of course not!*

**Metal Coins, c. 640 BC, Lydia (Ancient Turkey)**

*A coin for your thoughts!*

Telescope: Hans Lippershey, 1608, the Netherlands

Microscope: Hans and Zacharias Janssen, c. 1600, the Netherlands

## KARL BENZ: Motorcar, 1885, Germany

*Faster!*

*Left, please.*

*Too late!*

In 1888, Mrs. Benz borrowed her husband's tri-wheel motorcar without permission! She drove over 75 miles. It was the first long-distance journey by car.

### EDWARD NAIME
Eraser, 1770, Great Britain
*I'm nothing without you!*

*I'm nothing without you!*

### BARDEEN, BRATTAIN, and SHOCKLEY
Transistor, 1948, USA

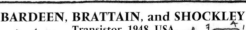

A transistor is an electronic device used as a switch to control or amplify an electric current. Without it, many modern gadgets would not be possible.

Telescope, microscope, spectacles — I'm still as blind as a bat!

### ARISTOPHANES of Byzantium
Punctuation, c. 200 BC

*Brilliant!*

*\* :: -*

**Mirror, c. 2500 BC, Ancient Egypt**

*Mirror, mirror, on the wall . . .*

*Best not to ask!*

Strange!

# Ring Those Bells for Antonio Meucci (1808–1889), Alexander Graham Bell (1847–1922), and the Telephone

Antonio Meucci was a wealthy and successful Italian inventor living in Cuba. In 1849, while he was trying out a new electrotherapy device on a friend, he heard him cry out from an adjoining room. The sound had been carried along the wires. He realized that he had discovered a way to transmit the human voice.

A year later, Antonio and his wife, Esther, left Cuba for Staten Island, in New York.

Here Antonio worked on many inventions, including the one he called his telettrofono.

But he soon began to run out of money, partly because he was so generous to fellow Italians.

Antonio had set up a telettrofono between his house and workshop so his wife could call him in an emergency. In 1860, he demonstrated the system to local journalists and wealthy businessmen. He hoped to raise money to develop it.

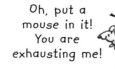
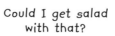

*Great invention, old buddy!*

*But I was hoping for a little investment.*

*Care for lunch?*

**But Antonio's English was weak, and he could not persuade anyone to back his invention.**

*What if someone steals my idea?*

House SOLD

*We'll have lost everything.*

**Worse still, he was now so poor he could not afford to register a patent to protect his idea.**

*Not the telettrofono?*

*I'm sorry, sweetheart. There was no other way. You were hurt and I was starving.*

**When he was injured in an explosion, Esther sold his telephone models to pay his medical bills.**

*I'm sure it will work.*

*Looks interesting.*

**When he recovered, Antonio quickly made another prototype and asked the Great Western Union telegraph company for permission to test it on their telegraph wires.**

*Just leave it with us, sir.*

*Of course we haven't forgotten!*

*No decision yet, sir.*

*Maybe next week!*

*Come back tomorrow!*

*He's busy today.*

*Appointment, sir?*

*Not in!*

*I'm busy!*

*Come back after Thanksgiving.*

*We meant next Thanksgiving!*

*It's lost!*

**They kept the prototype and promised to get back to him, but they never did. Antonio visited their offices almost every week for two years. Finally, he was told that the prototype was lost.**

**Meanwhile, other inventors were catching up to Antonio. One was a Scotsman, Alexander Graham Bell.**

*The boy's a genius!*

*Faster! Faster!*

A MACHINE FOR DEHUSKING WHEAT

**As a child, Alexander was interested in inventing and in his father's work as a teacher of the deaf.**

*A genius! A genius!*

*How are you, Grandmother?*

*A talking dog! What next?*

**Alexander experimented with teaching his pet dog to speak by manipulating its vocal chords. He was quite successful!**

Can I have a talking dog?

Sorry, not at home . . . please leave a message.

21

Inventors invent. Birds chirp. It's the way the world works.

Alexander called his first machine a harmonic telegraph.

The first telephones worked on private circuits that ran from house to house.

By the 1880s, more than 50,000 Americans owned telephones!

Slurp!

By the time he was 26, Alexander and his family had moved to Canada.

Alexander later went on to tutor teachers of deaf people in Boston. Here he met his future wife, Mabel Hubbard.

Alexander spent his spare time trying to invent a telephone, but without much success.

Then Mabel's father gave him money to employ a technician named Tom Watson.

Alexander and Tom experimented with different speech machines day and night.

On February 14, 1876, Mabel's father felt they were close to success and registered a patent.

On March 10, their big moment came. Alexander talked into their latest transmitter, and Tom heard him on a receiver in the other room. Their telephone worked!

A tortoise can no more help not inventing than he can help not thinking.

Thinking is not like eating — you don't have to think to live.

22

**Alexander quickly started to work on improving his model and on selling the idea. He even traveled to England to demonstrate his telephone to Queen Victoria.**

Is that what's known as a long-distance call?

**But not everyone was happy. Antonio Meucci was sure that his idea had been stolen. He protested in newspapers and in the courts until he died, in poverty, in 1889.**

Bell made the first long-distance call in 1892.

You'll be talking mobile phones next!

**There were other cases too. There was even one against the Great Western Union, who had employed Thomas Edison to make a telephone system for them. Alexander began to tire of the time he had to spend on protecting his patent. In 1879, now rich and famous, he went back to helping deaf students and inventing other things.**

Mobile phones: 1947

**The latest twist in the story came in 2002, when the U.S. Congress decided that the true inventor of the telephone was Antonio Meucci. But many people still believe that it was Alexander's enthusiasm for the telephone, as well as his ability to communicate, that convinced people it was a great idea.**

What's an inventor without money?

A forgotten inventor.

Ring-a-ling! Ring-a-ling!

I have a ringing in my ears—first it's light pollution and then it's noise pollution.

Wan Hoo of China invented a flying machine in AD 1500 — it exploded!

Hot-air balloonists were the first airmen.

As children, Wilbur and Orville Wright loved to make and invent things—especially things that flew. In their hometown of Dayton, Ohio, they earned pocket change by selling their creations.

Later, they opened a bicycle shop together. Bicycles were just becoming popular, and they grew skilled at repairing and building them.

When they read about the death of the pioneer glider Otto Lilienthal in 1896, they became determined to build their own flying machine!

Hot-air balloons often exploded!

I only explode if there is a worm shortage.

Otto Lilienthal made more than 2,000 successful glider flights before his fatal accident.

After much research, they built a glider and flew it—as a kite! Then they started planning a glider that could carry a person.

In 1900 and 1901, they tested two full-size gliders, but neither was a success. The brothers almost gave up.

Keep your feet firmly on the ground— that's my advice!

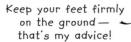

Keep your feet inside your shell and your shell on the ground—that's mine.

Instead, they went back to work. They built a wind tunnel and tested different wing shapes.

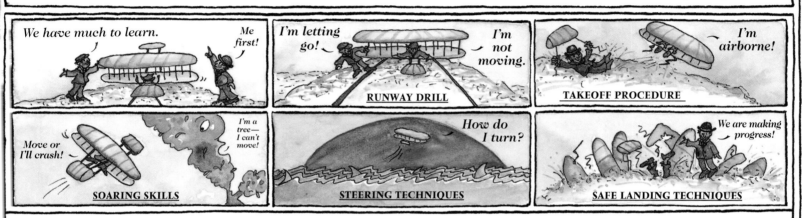

Their third glider was a great success, and the brothers made nearly a thousand glides in it. Then they started to build their first fully powered airplane with its own engine and propellers.

By the end of 1903, they were ready to fly. On December 17, at Kill Devil Hill, near Kitty Hawk, North Carolina, Orville launched himself into the air in their airplane, *Flyer 1*, and flew for 12 seconds. It was the first powered flight ever!

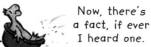

Over the next two years, Wilbur and Orville built two more planes, constantly improving their designs. By 1905, *Flyer 3* could stay in the air more than 30 minutes, turning and looping at speeds of up to 35 mph.

26

Then in 1908, after signing a contract with the U.S. War Department, Wilbur toured France and America to demonstrate his flying invention. In New York, he flew around the Statue of Liberty to the amazement of the crowds below. Wilbur and Orville had conquered the air!

# Viva, Guglielmo Marconi
## (1874–1937)
## and His Radio

What are radio waves and what do they do?

James Maxwell discovered them in 1864; Heinrich Hertz produced them in 1883.

They carry signals, such as sounds, through the air at the speed of light!

Through the air? Like us?

Yes, but invisibly!

Scary!

PING! POW! ZAP!

*Mr. Franklin will now prove that lightning has electric power!*

*Grr!*

*Clever boy!*

*A stint in the Navy is what you need, my boy.*

**As a boy, Guglielmo irritated his Italian father by pretending to be the scientist Benjamin Franklin and experimenting with the power of lightning.**

*Listen, Mama, I can make the bell ring without wires!*

*Late one night . . .*

*Radio Waves*

*Is it magic, dear?*

*WOOF?*

*Radio Waves*

*BE QUIET! I'm trying to sleep.*

*PING!*

BATTERY    SPARK PRODUCER

TRANSMITTER

BATTERY

RECEIVER

**Then he read about the work of Heinrich Hertz on electromagnetic waves. Guglielmo realized that the waves could be used to send messages without a wire between the sender, or the transmitter, and the receiver. He became completely absorbed by the idea and repeated Hertz's experiments many times at home.**

*Are you waving or playing?*

*Shhh, pet, I'm resting!*

*Silly, nonsense! Be QUIET!*

**His brother, Alfonso, helped. He would wait in their garden with a receiver and wave a handkerchief when he received messages sent by Guglielmo from the attic.**

*Ah, gunshot! He's heard my signal!*

*AERIAL*

*TAP-TAP-TAP!*

BANG!

*Be QUIET!*

**Soon Guglielmo was sending messages to Alfonso over longer distances.**

28

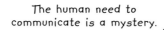
The human need to communicate is a mystery.

BURP!

Crumbs! Will it be wireless telephones next? Where will I perch?

Did you mention crumbs?

Any more crumbs and you'll need the Wright brothers to get you airborne!

He tried to interest the Italian post office in his experiments, but they were not interested.

Guglielmo set sail for England, where their postal service gave him money and technical help.

We all need a helping hand at times.

His experiments went well, and in 1897, he had founded the Wireless Telegraph and Signal Company Ltd. They were producing radios by 1898. In 1909, when the SS *Republic* collided with another ship, radio communication saved almost all the passengers—more than 1,700 people.

First transatlantic signal: Guglielmo Marconi, 1901, Italy

In 1898, Queen Victoria used wireless radio to communicate with the royal yacht.

Guglielmo returned to Italy as a hero. Before long, new uses were found for radio waves, helped by the invention of valves that made it easier to detect and transmit radio waves clearly. In the 1920s, radio stations such as the BBC started entertainment broadcasting, but Guglielmo was not impressed. He wanted his wireless radio to save lives at sea and believed all other uses were frivolous.

The wireless telegraph saved its first life at sea in 1899.

SPLASH!

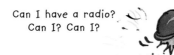
Can I have a radio? Can I? Can I?

Dream on!

29

# Tune In for JOHN LOGIE BAIRD (1888–1946) and the TV BOYS

John Logie Baird was fascinated by new inventions. While still a schoolboy, he connected his house in Scotland to his friends' houses with a homemade telephone exchange (although the wires that he hung across the road were a little too low!). Later his interest turned to television.

John was determined to be the first to make a working television. But the system he chose was very different from the electronic TV of today. His system was mechanical and used huge spinning disks to generate a tiny picture. He had no money, so he had to build it in his kitchen out of old junk.

Sometimes the disks spun out of control, showering the room with glass and metal. But John did not give up.

In 1925, in a London department store, he became the first person to demonstrate a mechanical television.

A year later, a group of scientists lined up outside John's tiny kitchen to watch him demonstrate his TV system. They loved it, and soon John was able to persuade the British Broadcasting Corporation to show experimental TV programs.

But, unfortunately for John, the mechanical system was not as good as the electronic system that other inventors were working on at the same time. Philo T. Farnsworth, a farmer's son from Utah, was the first person to suggest an electronic system in 1922, when he was only 14 years old.

It was Japanese inventor Kenjiro Takayanagi who demonstrated the first fully electronic televisions in 1926. But the inventor who helped make TV possible was a Russian American, Vladimir Zworykin, who developed equipment that recorded images and displayed pictures. This was the birth of television as we know it today! By the 1950s, TV sets were starting to appear in every home—thanks to the enthusiasm and hard work of these inventors and many others just like them.

# Extra-Loud Cheer for WOMEN INVENTORS

## STEPHANIE KWOLEK: Kevlar, 1966, USA

Kevlar is an exceptionally strong plastic material. Used in radial tires and knife- and bulletproof vests, it has saved MANY lives!

## QUEEN LEIZU
### Silk, c. 3200 BC, China

In early times, if you wanted to be known as a female inventor, it helped to be a queen.

## BEULAH HENRY
**Snap-on Umbrella Cover and other inventions, 1912–1970, USA**

Beulah held 49 patents. She is sometimes known as "Lady Edison."

## MELITTA BENTZ
**Coffee Filter Papers, 1908, Germany**

## SARAH E. GOODE
**Folding Cabinet Bed, 1885, USA**

Sarah was the first African American woman to receive a patent in the United States.

## AYME BALL
**Preserved Saffron, 1637, Great Britain**

Ayme Ball was a widow when she became the first woman to be granted her own patent.

## REBECCA CHING
**Worm-Destroying Lozenge, 1796, Great Britain**

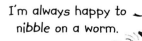

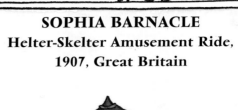

## ROSE MITCHTOM
### Teddy Bear, 1902, USA

*Are you a honeybee?*

*No, I'm your president.*

## MARGARETE STEIFF
### Teddy Bear, 1902, Germany

*For you, Auntie!*

*This will make a great cuddly toy.*

Both Rose and Margarete have a claim to the teddy bear. Rose named hers after the U.S. president Teddy Roosevelt, when he refused to shoot a baby bear. Margarete's was based on a nephew's drawing.

## SARAH MATHER
### Submarine Telescope and Lamp, 1845 and 1870, USA

*Blistering barnacles! If only I'd had a Sarah Mather telescope!*

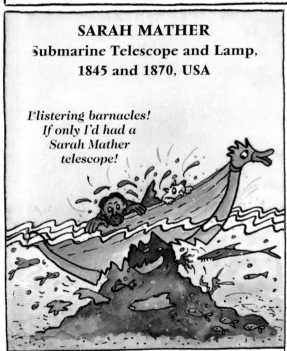

The telescope and lamp allowed vessels to survey the ocean depths.

## ANN MOORE
### Snugli, 1969, USA

*Translated, that means "I want a Snugli."*

*Waaa!*

*Coo-Coo!*

**Ann invented the Snugli after a visit to West Africa.**

## ISABELLA CUNIO
### Woodblock Engraving, c. 1200, Italy

*Brother, let's carve the exploits of Alexander into wood, then dip them in ink and print them.*

*Okay, but only if I take the credit, 'cause I'm the boy!*

**It is likely that Isabella made the first known woodblock engravings with her twin, Alex.**

## MARY ANDERSON
### Windshield Wiper, 1903, USA

*Maybe I should invent a windshield wiper.*

*Keep on wiping!*

## SOPHIA BARNACLE
### Helter-Skelter Amusement Ride, 1907, Great Britain

*WEE!*

*WOOAH!*

*ZOOM!*

*FASTER!*

*Me, me! Me next!*

*Is it safe?*

A PENNY A TURN!

The teddy bear is one of the most popular toys ever invented.

Has anyone invented a birdie-bear?

Another bird-brain!

If my mom had used a Snugli, I might have grown into a dove!

Even a Snugli can't work miracles!

Unlike women inventors and owl brains!

## FRANCES GABE
**Self-Cleaning House, 1950, USA**

**Everything got washed in Frances's house: dishes, books, even the dog!**

## JAN VAN EYCK
**Oil Paints, c. 1410, Flanders**

*These are some of my best colors!*

**Watercolor paints, invented by the Chinese c. AD 900, are incredible too.**

## UNKNOWN DUTCH INVENTOR
**Roller Skates, c. 1700**

*Don't stop playing!*

**In 1760, Joseph Merlin wore a pair to a ball in London. While playing the violin, he crashed into a mirror!**

## JOHN STARLEY
**Safety Bicycle, 1885, Britain**

*Bikes came in all shapes until I invented the safety bike!*

**The first known bicycle was invented in 1817, by Baron von Drais of Germany.**

## JOHAN VAALER
**Paper Clip, 1899, Norway**

*A small, but perfect, design.*

## JOHN MONTAGU, FOURTH EARL OF SANDWICH
**The Sandwich, 1762, Great Britain**
YUM!  YUM!

## WALTER HUNT
**Modern Safety Pin, 1849, USA**

*An Ancient Egyptian invented the first safety pin, of course!*

## ANCIENT ROMANS
**Cross-Bladed Scissors, ages ago! (c. AD 100)**

*Perfect for cutting toenails or paper or hair or cheese or . . .*

## RICHARD KNERR AND ARTHUR MERLIN
**First Plastic Hula-Hoop, 1958, USA**

**A toy that originally came from Ancient Egypt.**

## LU PAN
**Kite, c. 400 BC, China**

## OLE KIRK CHRISTIANSEN
**Lego, 1955, Denmark**

*I made it myself!*

My favorite invention is my shell.

I'm with you, Dad — "Ever inward" is my motto.

## JACOB FUSSELL
### Factory-made Ice Cream, 1851, USA

The first handmade ice cream may have been made in Persia about 100 BC.

## CONRAD GESNER
### Pencil, 1565, Germany

Conrad invented a wood and graphite pencil, but English shepherds were the first to write with graphite.

## CHRISTIAN BERNHARD TAUCHNITZ
### Paperback Book, 1841, Germany

## ADOLPHE SAX
### Saxophone, 1846, Belgium

## JOHN WALKER
### Matches, 1827, Great Britain

## GLAMOROUS WOMEN OF ANCIENT EGYPT
### Cosmetics, c. 3000 BC

## JOSEPH N. NIEPCE
### Photography, 1826, France

By 1839, Louis Daguerre from France and William Fox Talbot from England had developed systems that improved on Joseph's process.

## OWEN MACLAREN
### Baby Stroller, 1965, Great Britain

Q: Why a baby stroller?
A: Because it has a baby in it!

## MARVIN STONE
### Drinking Straw, 1888, USA

No drink is complete without one!

## FRANÇOIS LOUIS CAILLER
### Chocolate Bar, 1819, Switzerland

Hernán Cortés, the Spanish explorer, brought the cocoa bean to Europe from Mexico in 1519. It was the beginning of all things chocolate! Thank you, Hernán!

Alcock, Walter  18
Anderson, Mary  33
Aristophanes of Byzantium  19

Baird, John Logie  30–31
Ball, Ayme  32
Bardeen, John  19
Barnacle, Sophia  33
Bell, Alexander Graham  4, 20–23
Bentz, Melitta  32
Berg, Madame  26
Benz, Karl  19
Berners-Lee, Tim  19
Birdseye, Clarence  18
Biro, Ladislao  18
Booth, Hubert  19
Brattain, Walter  19

Cailler, François Louis  35
Cayley, George  7
Chappe, Claude  16
Ching, Rebecca  32
Christiansen, Ole Kirk  34
Cunio, Isabella  33

da Vinci, Leonardo  6–7
Daguerre, Louis  35
de L'Orme, Philibert  18
de Mestral, George  18
degli Armati, Salvino  19
di Spina, Alessandro  19
Dickson, Earle  18
Drebbel, Cornelis  7
Durand, Peter  18

Edison, Thomas  16–17, 23
Engelbart, Doug  19

Farah, Abdul  34
Farnsworth, Philo T.  31
Focke, Heinrich  7
Franklin, Benjamin  28
Fussell, Jacob  35

Gabe, Frances  34
Gesner, Conrad  35
Gifford, Henri,  25
Goldmark, Peter  31
Goode, Sarah E.  32
Gutenberg, Johannes  10–11

Harrington, John  18
Henlein, Peter  19
Henry, Beulah  32
Hero of Alexandria  12
Hertz, Heinrich  28
Hill, Rowland  18
Higginbotham, Will  19
House, Kenneth  19
Hunt, Walter  34
Hyatt, John  35

Ibuka, Masaru  19

Janssen, Hans  19
Janssen, Zacharias  19
Jobs, Steve  19
Judson, Whitcomb  19

Kilby, Jack  19
Knerr, Richard  34
Kwolek, Stephanie  32

Leizu, Queen  32
Lenormand, Louis  7
Lilienthal, Otto  24
Lippershey, Hans  19
Lu Pan  34

Maclaren, Owen  35
Marconi, Guglielmo  4, 28–29
Mather, Sarah  33
Merlin, Arthur  34
Meucci, Antonio  20–23
Mitchtom, Rose  33
Montagu, John  34
Moore, Ann  33
Morse, Samuel  16

Naime, Edward  19
Newcomen, Thomas  12
Niepce, Joseph N.  35
Nipkow, Paul  30
Noyce, Robert  19

Pi Sheng  10
Popov, Aleksandr  30

Sax, Adolphe  35
Semmelweis, Ignaz  18
Sheffield, Dr. Washington  18
Shockley, William  19
Smith, Randolph  19
Starley, John  34
Steiff, Margarete  33
Stephenson, George  14–15
Stone, Marvin  35
Strite, Charles  19
Sundback, Gideon  19
Swan, Joseph  17

Takayanagi, Kenjiro  31
Talbot, William Fox  35
Tauchnitz, Christian Bernhard  35
Trevithick, Richard  14–15

Vaaler, Johan  34
van Eyck, Jan  34
von Drais, Baron  34

Walker, John  35
Wan Hoo  24
Watt, James  12–13, 14
Wozniak, Stephen  19
Wright, Orville and Wilbur  7, 24–27, 29

Yeates, Robert  18

Zworykin, Vladimir  31

# Index of Inventions

antenna 30
airplane 7, 24–27
alphabet 8
antiseptics 18

baby stroller 35
ballpoint pen 18
Band-Aid 18
bicycle 34
button 19

calendar 8
can opener 18
cast-iron rails 14
celluloid 35
chocolate bar 35
coffee filter papers 32
coins 19
computer games 19
computer mouse 19
concrete 18
cosmetics 35

drinking straw 35

electric light 16–17
encyclopedia 34
eraser 19
eyeglasses 19

frozen food 18
folding cabinet bed 32

glider 24–25

hang glider 7
helicopter 7
helter-skelter 33
Hula-Hoop 34

ice cream 35
ink 10

Kevlar 32
kite 34

Lego 34
light bulb 17

matches 35
microscope 19
miner's safety lamp 15
mirror 19
mobile phone 19, 23
Morse code 16
motorcar 19
mouthwash 18
movable type 10–11

Newcomen engine 12–13
Nipkow disk 30

oil paints 34

paper 10
paperback book 35
paper clip 34
parachute 7
pencil 35
personal computer 19
phonograph 17
photography 35
pop-up book 35
portable fire pump 14
postage stamp 18
preserved saffron 32
punctuation 19

radio 28–29
roller skates 34

safety pin 34
sandwich 34
saxophone 35
scissors 34
self-cleaning house 34
separate steam condenser 12–13
silicon chip 19
silk 32
sliced bread 19
smoke alarm 19
snap-on umbrella cover 32
Snugli 33
steam engine 12–13, 14
steam locomotive 14–15
steam railroad 14–15

steel rails 14
submarine 7
submarine lamp 33
submarine telescope 33

tank 7
teddy bear 33
telegraph 16
telephone 20–23
telescope 19
television 30–31
tin can 18
toaster 19
toilet 18
toilet paper 18
toothpaste 18
transistor 19

vacuum cleaner 19
Velcro 18

Walkman 19
World Wide Web 19
watch 19
watercolor paint 34
wireless telegraph 29
windshield wiper 33
worm-destroying lozenge 32
woodblock engraving 33

zipper 19